HOLE IN THE WALL

Also by Judi Benson

Poetry

Somewhere Else
(Turret Books, 1990)

In the Pockets of Strangers
(Rockingham Press, 1993)

Call It Blue
(Rockingham Press, 2000)

The Thin Places
(Rockingham Press, 2006)

Anthologies

Co-edited with Ken Smith, *Klaonica: Poems for Bosnia.*
(Bloodaxe Books, 1993)

Edited and produced, *What Poets Eat,*
food-related poems and recipes. (Foolscap, 1994)

Co-edited with Agneta Falk, *The Long Pale Corridor:
Contemporary Poems of Bereavement.* (Bloodaxe Books, 1996)

Edited, *Not Just Words: One Word Sonnets and Other Words,*
an anthology of patients' and staff' writing.
(Dumfries and Galloway Health Board with financial assistance
from the Scottish Arts Council, 2006)

Judi Benson

HOLE IN
THE WALL

Rockingham Press

Published in 2013 by
The Rockingham Press
11 Musley Lane,
Ware, Herts SG12 7EN
www.rockinghampress.com

British Library Cataloguing-in-Publication Data

A catalogue record for this book
is available from the British Library

ISBN 978-1-904851-50-9

Printed in Great Britain
by the MPG Group

Forget your perfect offering, there's a crack in everything, that's how the light gets in.

Leonard Cohen

Contents

Acknowledgements

Some of these poems have been published in the following: *Acumen, Ambit, Cold Shelter* (anthology "Floored Genius"), *Not Just Words: One Word Sonnets and Other Words* (anthology), *Stand, Sunk Island Review* podcast, *Tall Lighthouse*.

Green Gym

I can't hear the Great Spotted Woodpecker
for all this twitter, chitter, chatter, and what does it matter?
Deep breaths. This is as fresh as air gets around here,
near to but not quite the A something motorway.

This is where we come to get away from all that bogs us down;
our bit of wilderness to tend, amongst the tombstones.
We bend Hazel branches, weave them to make a dead hedge,
a home for Voles, Stag Beetles, the Slow Worm which isn't.

We've sawn down the branches, strimmed the leaves,
hammered in the posts we chiseled to a point.
Through the mud and the slush and the hush
of the dead around us, we work.

Through the rain and the sleet, in the wind,
dodging hail stones or in a breathless heat we meet.
Our task? Don't ask.
None too great, none too small, like us.

Through the ice and a slice of sorrow that cuts us
as finely as chisel on stone, we carry on.
A name, a date, a story told again in our uncovering –
Albert, hidden for a hundred years, alone, no other names.

We try to imagine him at thirteen, cause of death and if an accident.
Did the family move away, die of grief, hunger, disease, old age?
Each of us has our talents, our limitations, our altercations.
But whatever greyness we come with, whatever angst,

we leave a little rosier, subdued and silent for a moment. That quiet
that comes when we're engaged, focused on hauling barrows
of steaming mulch, raking the falling leaves, sawing a trunk
of ivy off a tree, kindred, amongst the spirits, the Robin's song.

Hammered

Just
when
you
think
you've
got
it
nailed
down,
you
find
you've
been
screwed.

Taxing Times

The petty piddling of it all, ins and outs, pence and pounds,
the, *I owe, you owe me;* trying to keep things even,
when there's no way to repay.

Even in death's yawning eye, you worried about money.
Is there enough to pay for all this? Wasted breath
we might have saved, for all the things we can't say now.

So I got a sea bream, thought of cooking it.
Taxes took the taste away. Dead money, that's all there is.
I do declare, and declare every ream of paper a dead-end.

I don't earn but I work hard at proving it.
Here's the proof of my failings,
how I've lived my life all wrong.

See the doughnut, see the hole.
My profits are there in the middle,
where the jam ought to be.

Certain Uncertainties

I know I'm alive, due to catch the 10:45 from Euston.
I don't know that the tube will get me there in time,
or if the Instant Ticket will slot out of the machine.

Everything is running away; gums from teeth, money from account.
All future prospects suffering from drought.
What a fat juicy word for such shriveled dryness.

I don't know that I'll find the Reserved seat or if it will be Facing.
I don't know that the loo will be working, the Buffet open.
I know my luggage won't fit in Virgin's rack, size of a Tampax.

I can't predict who will sit next to me; I won't be smoking, or talking.
I don't know I'll make the Carlisle connection. Don't know that I won't.
And if I make it to Dumfries, will it be pissing down, no room in the Inn.

The Hoose I've looked for only exists in cyber space, as if I'd made it up.
I can't know what I'll be like there,
what the weather will do to my hair.

If only the world was flat, I could just walk off the edge, plop.
But it's not, so round and round I go,
as if I'll ever catch my tail before the tale gets told.

Beware the Fat Lady. Don't give her the mike.

The Set-Up

My office is down below, where Danger Trolleys live,
near to but not quite the Morgue,
every door Alarmed about something.
Engine of the beast, belly of the great ship Hope.
It sails in its own galaxy, a lighthouse gleaming through the dark.
Warning, warning, don't crash on these rocks.
Hospitals are dangerous places, the usual suspects:
Pseudomonas, klebsiella, streptoccus, protens, e-coli,
 staph aureus, Norovirus, MRSA, C. difficile, and all the rest,
waiting to create themselves.
Every corridor is a labyrinth, Mediaeval,
mirroring the layout of the town.
It's a maze that could lose you. Don't let it.
Each will take you to a different world,
spinning another tale to ensnare you.
I rescued this fox cub, kin?, so small
my wee son held it in his hands, kin?
I raised her, called her Minky, the Stinky.
You don't know the rules, only that they're easy to break.
It's like skipping rope. You have to know when it's safe to jump in.
Safe? Never, just lesser and greater dangers.
Are you my mother, the one of ninety-two asks, as I pass by,
another woman calling out,
My husband would have paid good money for you.
The machinery grunts and grinds to its own rhythm.
You'll find another language is spoken here, doctor says.
Don't try to learn it or else you'll forget your own.
Eat all the apples you like, we'll still come,
swinging our stethoscopes. They're hard to come by.
See, mine's purple, distinctive.

Phlebotomist
(for Cath Carrick)

She didn't lie in bed at night as a wee lassie,
stroking her arms, trying to find veins in the dark.

She didn't dream rivers tentacled with veins,
try to follow their threaded tributaries,

measuring the rise and fall of the elusive blue line.
If Vamperine dreams she had, she never was a blood sucker,

just the sleeping bride, no blood on her lips.
She wasn't keen on needles, not a masochist, not a sadist,

did nae want to hurt anyone, not poke, prick, stab,
jab panic into their faces. No pins in dolls.

She didn't say *when I grow up*... Just one idle day,
flipping through the ads, circles one. *That sounds different.*

Not knowing what a difference she'd make.
Master now, she's Sister Haematology's right arm and both of yours.

Tap, tapping like a miner, getting rivers of blood to flow,
finding gold slivers of veins, where were none.

The Blanket

I call this one the Merry square, though she's not always,
and no one would call her square.

Grey, finely spun yarn she gives me.
I knit in a zig-zag moss stitch.

Patience, I say, this is a difficult pattern.
Hairy days she has between treatments.

The bones, the joints, the ache, the burning feet,
tingle in the fingertips, heart burn, breathlessness.

Mouth like *the bottom of the biscuit tin.* Thrush,
fever rush, a restlessness with no energy for anything.

But she's up and down anyway, hands in and out the water,
dry skin cracking. Her man indoors she wishes was nae.

Sleepless nights on steroids, waking at half two, three.
Ovaltine, the sound of her spoon waking the birds.

Might as well get a night job. Dreich days, fair scunnered days,
smirrie rain, wind whistling through the wig she wears less and less.

She's ready to go before she's sat down. Keep a check
on the tension. Don't let this yarn snap.

She tugs on her wooly hat, brushing it all aside.
Just look arounds, she says, *always someone worse off.*

In and Out the Alex Unit
(i.m. For Marion)

I tell her, all you have to do is sit still,
surrender your fingertips, your nails, for Nurse
to shape and polish, while you gaze at the bird feeder,
hanging from a branch of the Beech tree.
Cars, people coming and going, some you know.
Hello, you whisper, warm behind the chilled glass.
Helicopter on the landing pad, stirring up the frosty grass.
And the not so far away hills changing colour in the light,
sun russing up the tree tops as it sinks, slowly.
And Robin, dear Robin, puffing up against the cold,
nuts too tightly packed. Every day he tries.

Inside, prunes in a basket. The gaudy pink, disjointed fairy,
dangling, jumping about when you don't want her to. Sleepiness
when you long to be awake. Wakefulness,
when you long for sleep. Your body all jiggered.
Midazolam, Propofal, fancy names for things
that mess up your mind, pluck at your imaginings.
That concentrated furrow of the brow, those busy hands
clutching at air, arranging, re-arranging, trying to put things
to rights in this world, when there is no right,
just wrong and wrong again,
round the roundabout with only one exit.

Seasoned

Horse Chestnuts are the first to go, golden leaves.
Then Sycamore, contrasts, crimson,
Plasma one drop every fifteen seconds.
Iron to red and back again, all the stages between.
Chartreuse, ochre, platelets.
I am leafing through changes,
picking up the fallen ones.
Mystery tours, on, off the grounds, or just,
Look at that brushstroke, yellow dabbling with green.
Look at the light. Listen.
Never again that leaf to fall.
Never again that leaf.

In A Word

I love the way the trees say *Aye,*
as they fling their leaves,
confetti at my feet.

Not a dainty Highland fling of a word
but a booming sound that comes from the roots,
groins its way up through bark,

rumbles in the throat awhile, then bursts forth
emphatically, *Aye,* sending a percussion
of colours to clash.

The gulls are frantic with it,
Aye,aye,aye, circling the swirl of leaves,
spent now, gold covering the green.

Bird's Eye

My day begins with copulation,
lying on my back studying clouds,
watching gulls on the rooftop across the way.
Oh they've got their foreplay,
as close as beak-ed things come to kissing.
Peck-pecking, doing a dainty dance around
each other in that almost-touching flamenco way.
As close as they get to hugging, and so and so.
Tap tap, slap slap on the tiles awhile,
then *enough of that,* as he takes off, graceful lands atop her,
a showy span of white wing,
doing the jiggery-pokery thing.
She's uninvolved, looking down at her feet,
thinking she needs to see a podiatrist, psychiatrist.
It's all too much,
all this fuss and feathers
just to end up sitting on a nest
like all the rest. Common, one of the flock.

Snaps

Twenty-five photographs and not a single word for it.
Some bird twittering, white geese on a green field.
How to capture the blankness of sky, what to do with it.
Not a single break in the foggy mist.

I stride along the path beneath the bower of leaves,
my gait smooth as that duck's glide on the glassy-eyed Nith.
And so the green blinds me, refusing to name itself.
The Galloway hills roll and roll trying to rise above the mist.

The river runs its reflections of spectacular trees,
Each a tangle of branches with leaves stuck on, competing
to be the brightest ones. Light, air, Siberian geese
struggling towards an alphabet only sky can read.

Yes, my eyes are assaulted with all this, and pine too.
But what's it matter without you.
I'd say, *Look at the smoky mist.*
And you'd say, *I'm part of that mist now.*

Disgruntled Daff of Dumfries

I'm fair scunnered, always having to be bright,
stand up straight, crisply kinked, just so.
Jolly jonquil trumpeting my arrival,
only to hear the punters say,
Gosh, the daffs are early this year.

O to be a daffodil in springtime, the minstrels sing,
as if it's easy, head-butting the frozen ground.
All that stretching, only to have your head lopped off
by a couple of yobs. Anyway, I've never liked yellow,
not even tinged with orange.

A powdery perfume that gets up my nose.
O the tedium, every year same again, more and more of us.
Next year I'm gonna split, join the winter pansies,
purple, floppy, velvety, no ironing, mean-faced as I feel.
Now that'd be a turnip for the gardeners.

Hole in the Wa'

Enough
of
alcohol
gel,
a
clean
diet
in
a
no
smoke
antiseptically
sterile
environment.

No.
I'll
go
doun
the
toon
to
Hole
in
the
Wa,
boost
my
immunity.

Den
of
smokequidity,
alcohol
gulped
down,
inside.
Tiger
Lil
taking
a
spill
stool
and

all.
Buzz
that
dancin'
fool,
crooning
to
the
partner
he
thinks
his
arms
hold.

A Perfect Day for Drowning

Yesterday I'd have been happy to be blown off the path
into the swirling Nith, let myth make of me an explanation.
Today's not one of those days, though more likely to happen.
See how the black bird struggles against the wind.
Again and again she gets a running start, flaps her wings,
hurls herself into the air, only to be knocked back sideways.
I know how she feels. She's at the end of her invisible tether,
a worm dangling at the end of her beak.
Worm is betting on the wind, the bird's impatience,
that moment when she opens her beak to squawk
at things not going her way. Even the air lets her down.
Maybe tomorrow will be a more perfect day for drowning,
no bird or worm to distract me.

Clinic in November

Late afternoon, all day pinned down by a line
to the juices that fix you with their poisons.
Mine's hamster juice, he says,
Mine's periwinkle, says she, fluttering her pink eyelashes.
Early darkening of the sky,
a drop in temperature.
I'm always last, next time I'll come in pajamas, bring a torch.
Even the jokes have chilled. The closer it comes
to getting unhooked, the greater the agitation.
four men tapping their free hands on the sides of their chairs,
not even aware of the rhythm they have created.
Back ache, stiff legs, crabbit.
I wish I had a key to wind up my legs.
Twilight brings unwanted thoughts,
What if the treatment doesn't work?
Weary of the worry, wanting someone to hold your head
until all the thoughts run away to blank.

Mistaken

I'm not the lady with the phone card,
the taxi driver with the platelets from Glasgow,
the donor you've been praying for, or your transport home.
I'm not the wig lady with your long-awaited,
not a doctor, not a nurse, not a social worker,
not a carer, though I do.
I've not come to canulate you, take your blood,
bring the results you need.
I'm not the bag of pills you've waited for half the day.
I'm not the one thickening the soup with lentils.
I've not got the dinner trolley or your Daily Mail.
I'm not a joiner, the locksmith, the larky one
dusting around your bed. I'm not the receptionist
who's found your medical records, your X-rays.
I've got no answers, solutions, wonder drugs,
nothing useful, not even tap dancing.
I'm just the round woman sitting in a corner,
resident nutter, knitting helplessness into squares for a blanket.
Knitting, knotting, pearling thoughts, offering all I can.
Cup of tea? Coffee? Caterpillar sonnet,
Little Ladders of meaning,
basket weaving where no rushes go.

The Death Sentence

You've not murdered anyone, no grievous bodily harm,
No arson or armed robbery
but you've been given the death sentence. Nothing definite
like 12th of June by lethal injection at 10 a.m. Just a vague,
year or less or more, and that's your hope snuffed. You won't see
twenty-one, won't get a bus pass, no letter from the Queen.

There's no chance of appeal, re-stating your case, Plea
Bargaining, declaring innocence. No hung jury, no re-trial,
no reprieve and no choice: death by firing squad, hanging,
electrocution, guillotine. It's not an old black and white movie
where you see the Warden pick up the phone, glance at the clock,
in time to stay the execution. No, this is the body's clock,

some wily cells on the loose like Saturday night hooligans,
rampaging through your system, smashing platelets,
sitting on your blood count, stifling your breath,
gasping you with pain, sucking up the good cells,
erasing your immunity, turning your body against you.
And you wonder what you ever did to get your blood so angry.

Message to Joe

Backside a pin cushion, mirroring the same black purple,
on your arms, the oh so slow drip, drop, plop of the transfusion
that wears out your patience. *Now I kin why they call us patients.*
Be quicker to drink it. Seven years coming here to gain two.
Days hooked up to immobility, tiredness, one-handed,
flipping through the local paper, ear-phoned to the radio.
It helps to pass the time, killing the time it takes to buy some more.
You're running out of time, blood, options, fight,
though never humour. *Three buckets of blood*
and still my count's down. What's gaen on here,
must be a leak somewhere.
We all stared, looking for the leak we'd gladly have plugged.

P.S.
I found a nice pear, just the way you like it, off a tree.
And yes, duck eggs from the wild, not yin of those at the butcher's.
And a snow globe with music,
like the one you were always winding up on the ward
just as you did all of us.

The Changing Room

(For the Nurses at Dumfries and Galloway Royal Infirmary)

Natalie brings in the night air,
or early morning frost.
It melts in a gust of hospital heat.

She carries the river in her eyes,
wind tearing up the leaves. She carries her joy.
What she's seen fades in the glaring light.

Ursula takes off her jeans, wooly jumper,
Bling earrings, bits of herself,
sorrow for the death of her only child.

Rose folds away concerns for her mother
on another ward, whom she can't nurse.
Takes on thoughts of your mother, breathless.

She lets her name drop, to the badge on her pocket.
Nurse, nurse is the name she answers to.
She wishes she could clone herself.

Sandy suspends her body, the worrying lump in her breast,
tending to yours, lovingly. Anger is stuffed away
in some pocket, harsh words at home. Frustration,

the car that won't start, that she can't afford to replace,
her squeaky shoes from too many rain-drenched walks,
feeling faint and queasy all day long. All you see is *Nurse..*

You'll miss the moment of transformation. Emily
taking off her face, slipping into starched whites
tying her tresses back, affixing epaulets to her shoulders,

careful not to ruffle the feathers of her imaginary wings,
that give rise to you calling her *angel, angel,* she has to be.
That calm reassurance, easy smile, that touch of hers.

The way she treats you,
as if you're the only patient,
the ward, the only world she knows.

But she's no angel, this Nurse, Nurse, especially on her night off.
Her locker bulges with human frailties, simple needs,
sleep, food, love, shelter, chance of a fag, pockets of peace.

A Winter Moment

Last day of January, as if all the fug and funk will be gone tomorrow.
Soft frost, lining every blade of grass, etching bare branches.
Frozen ground, ice hanging at the base of drain pipes.
Dogs lick their bowls like lollies.

A slickery walk, black ice, not walking, sliding,
slipping, trying to skate uphill. Sky blanked out as if it's drunk
on frost, hills glittering like home-made Christmas cards.
And for a moment my heart is lifted by winter looking like itself.

Silence

You don't realise you've missed it until you get some.
That split second when the fridge stops refrigerating itself,
and the tick of your watch unwinds.
Channel Zero on the radio, just the buzzing of your thoughts,
looking for the words to say,
My ears are on holiday, per favore.

My Job?

Life,
to bring it in from the outside,
through dalelocks, o'er hillocks,
dodging bullocks of all kinds,
bringing armfuls of daffodils in photographs,
stream stopped in its chunter with my shutter.
A change of focus, shift of conversation beyond the medical.
How many stitches in a row?
Which bird is it that sings through the night?
Not Nightingale, too many letters. The thingamy, ken?
Try Robin. And who's running in the 4:30.
Forgetting for a moment to look at the clock,
the drip, the future, the disease
for which there is no cure.
Looking instead out the window,
blossom like snow flurries in a mild breeze.
Things forgotten float to the surface,
nostalgia, that other sickness.
Riding on father's shoulders,
that small, but tall enough to touch the branches.

Monday

You can't avoid it, always comes around again, whatever it calls itself, Wednesday, Sunday, the day you've been dreading, the cranking up again of all that noisy machinery you call your life, elusive, like a dog you call Saturday, that never comes. Or maybe it's just wash day, down by the riverside, snakes, crocs, rocks, beaten.

A Poem for Alex

they tried to grammarterise him
he'd have preferred to be glamourised
semi colon i don't even know where
my own fuckin colon is
commas full stops capital letters
just listen
you'll know when i'm finished

Naming

Go to the Mabie Forest and maybe you'll be inspired
by the lichen that likens itself to greeny sponge.
Give Biggar a miss; it's actually smaller.
Go back to Ae village, not unlike a village
you dreamt of when you were in your bucolic phase.
Oh it's miles away from Ware, which isn't just anywhere.
There the river runs swans and on every corner a pub;
moat town but not remote.

Love's Logic

That first winter
I thought of digging you up,
couldn't bear you down there shivering.
I was too mean in the end
to let you take the blanket I'd made.
Something from home, you'd said.
I'd get a spade and just…
What did I expect to find?

I've thought about that too,
and what if it's not you,
some other body or a box full of rocks –
Not box, bamboo, a basket,
as if you were a Moses baby
afloat in some state of drifting
down a slow ribbon of water,
in another world we can't see,
sunshine, leafy shade, shadows,
ribbles of wind, just there.

Wishful Thinking

I'm glad there wasn't a smoking ban,
those last luminous days, if they were to be my last.
Blushing like a girl at the waiter who bowed
when he brought the ash tray, winked,
or I blinked, imagined, sipped my wine,
flicked my ash, pen poised to capture snowflakes,
big as fifty pence pieces.
I will die in a snow storm, I wrote,
paused, flicked, didn't.

My Dumfries Garden

Three steep steps called stoop, where I may sit outdoors, risking piles,
landlady Audrey's garden being out of bounds, on account of the dog.
I only bought this place for the garden, then I got a dog. Max, you little...
I can't paint these rusty red steps blue or white, got to be in keeping
with the neighbourhood, though I can do what I like with the pots
on the sandstone graveled entrance. *Please yourself, Max will only*
dig them up again. Not on my watch, I whisper to the lobelia.

And always I'm in the wrong glint of the little sun at the time of day I like
to have a libation. Passers-by, cars in a hurry to Benvenito's, or using
Eastfield as a short-cut off the Annan Road. Well, I'm here anyway
for all the world to see, smoking, in my wrinkled clothes. *That writer perso*
working in the cancer ward. Madge next door, the widowed volunteer
at the hospital, clocks my absences in the sweetest manner. *I didn't see*
you, I wondered ..And I wonder why she's never there when I am.

I'm half here, half there, back home in my own space. Two roofs, one head
Too many chairs, too few glasses, for the two few to share.
Here the vista, there the canvas, cancelled out by a lack of time, space.
Half my heart's aloft, back in that room I created,
to get as close to clouds as I could. Days that's all there was,
clouds, canvas with nothing on. Here, street lights are the seasonal sun.
Days they never shut themselves off in the way I do.

Though I know but for clouds, all is luminous above. Back home,
there are places to take my restlessness, the jungle that the garden's become
in my absence. *You should go away more often*, I hear garden and foxes say
Now is the season of *can't see the neighbours, yet.* Not even the ghosts
have broken through. I'd hack back the St. John's Wort, good for depressio
an endorphin sandwich. I'd find again the path underneath the take-over vi
Mile a Minute, intertwined with Rosemary. I'd find my way to the shed

through the saw grass. Shadows of you would dart about,
turning my eye to the sockets of your masks, ivy poking through.
Don't cut that one, I'd hear you say about the bobble of a hydrangea
blocking the path. *I like the way it bounces when you brush past,*
a pom pom of white in the night.
I'm sitting on my rusty stoop in Dumfries and you're sitting on
the skinny planked, blue once red bench in the garden. *Move over.*

The Little Things

I'm
waiting
for
the
wisdom
my
years
have
accrued,
to
trickle
down,
influence
behaviour.
But
it's
only
me
again
in
my
Klondike
boots
trampling
the
Primulas.
Delicate
Heartsease
escapes
the
weeding
hand,
and
on
memory's
knees
I
weep
for
the
little
things
he
loved,
that
I
loved
his
loving
of.
A
caravan
wind,
he'd
say,
chimes.

Ode to My Own Bed

O mio letto,
let me lie down.
O downy soft me,
let me crib some sleep.

O cot, o cabin, o couchette, bassinette,
O cradle, let me down a rock
to log snore. Let me bed in you
O hammock, o futon, o fainting couch.

Let me slap a little dash
of sleep-eye, oh my.
O mio, o letto me pass out.
O pillow, o duvet, o quilt

O cotton sheets and all the sunshine
that dried you. O bedspread,
O blanket, the weight of it,
heavy, heavy lids, wanting nod.

O mattress, the bend of it
to my shape, the firm of it,
the soft of it, the spring
and the my of it.

O Morpheus come to me,
drown me with sleep
in your arms, in my bed
until my head awakes;

eyes left dreaming,
make believe landscapes,
seascapes, the boat, the man,
the bed again. O mio letto, let me go.

Waking Thought

If I didn't dream, I'd never see you.
There'd be no tenderness of touch
and all it leads to. There'd be no sea
lapping at my feet, no far off horizon,
if I didn't dream it up.
Nights when I don't dream, or don't remember,
there's such an emptiness, a hunger no food can fill.
All day my brain rumbles,
anticipating something I can't quite....

Crow

He thinks he's an acrobat, swinging back and forth,
back and forth, hanging by his feet to the thin wire.

I think he's someone's laundry on the line, swaying in a breeze.
We're both surprised when he up and flies away.

Dear Diary

What is this need of mine to tell you
all the daily bits and pieces, haps and misses.
The backed up drains, flooded washer, tiles off the roof,
me off my trolley, out on a razzle. And always it begins
with the weather as if I'm a meteorologist;
rain, sun, sleet, hail, gale, all in one day.

How much Ken's ears have been spared,
though he'd have tuned out, tuned into music,
which I'd have turned down so I could blether some more,
and furthermore. Up the volume, down the volume,
until I'd worn him out with my rattle,
all on the way to saying, *I love you, what would I do without you.*

Now I know and it doesn't amount to much,
just the same ole pottering about, one foot then the other,
washing the same clothes, same items on the grocery list,
minus the digestive biscuits,
though my hand still reaches for them,
along with the cat food for the long dead pets.

Some days I just want to lie down
on the floor of myself,
blend spine to wood plank,
become plankton,
a sea creature, Star fish.
Or something more weightless, air.

Thanks giving in Praha

Another riva, another walk along, alone,
keeping an eye out, eye in.
Roses, swans, ducks, dogs raising
their legs on the same spot.
Another set of candy colours
calling themselves buildings.
Willows weeping for no one, everyone.
Cobbles worn down by centuries of feet, hooves.
And what conversations transpired
here on these benches?
Secrets, lies, revolutions planned in whispers;
iron fist in a muffled glove,
sunshine crisp as hope.
Once you recognise the bridge
that crosses you home, you can relax,
let go of words like lost, lone, lament.
Listen, that thunder of tumbling water
could be the sea, and he...

Pistoia

The nose is wide awake with the scent
of all this flesh expanding me to fill
the spaces you left.
Even the tear ducts open wide now,
as if it's my job to fill the reservoirs, the au revoirs.
Riva, river, reiver, left behind on the other side
of this insurmountable mountain.
Oh grief, is there no end. No.
Another ring you left out, Dante.
And passion died and vision died,
and larking about died, and friends faded
as if you'd taken them with you,
leaving me twice as solo; widow woman,
as if I'm contagious, to be avoided.
Anyway, what about stars,
wishing I may, wishing I might,
first star of the night,
last table of poets in Pistoia,
coughing in the cobbled alley,
silent cigarettes.

Hotel Backwards

Please can you take me to Letoh Airtap.
I am a backwards thinking person,
trying to shade myself amongst a ruin of brick.
Beneath the leafy palm I sit, a bag of peaches
I still don't dare eat, my only clean dress,
and I far away from the country that adopted me,
gave me my red hair and the fiery temper to match.
I'm anxious to return to a recogniseable alone,
where there's no one to notice.
All the phone messages are automated,
selling package tours, two by two.
But you see, I'm ark-less and the sky is not infinite.
How thin the skin, how deep the bone.

After Siesta

I hang out the window, wanting to belong to this neighbouring hood
of houses, crammed back of Hotel Patria.
My geraniums, my nylons, cobalt blue net.
My mamma's, mamma's recipe, me shouting out
through the splintered blinds:
Ciao Gieusepple, comè stai, long time no...
Last year, this year's flowers.

Oh last year, what was that all about,
that ever after I've been trying to unpick.
The stitches of a life so carefully knitted.
Moth eaten now. What the hell, maybe it was me,
centuries ago, as tightly corseted in widow's needs.
The voyeur, not the participant. *Hello young lovers...*

I've sketched these balconies so many times,
I own them. That bowed-out bend of iron and I are intimate.
We keep bumping into each other.
The delicious crumble of it all. That's all it comes down to.
Cancel the starter, go for what you love, delicious crumble.

The Reckoning

People
tell
me
my
days
are
numbered;
always
have
been.
It's
called
a
calendar.

Specs

Worse things have happened.
Lost you didn't I?
But I can't read without them,
not even prices on packages,
and I can't afford another pair.
If only your old pair could show me
how you saw the world.
They didn't. So I chucked them,
found mine, lens up, glinting in the sun,
a step ahead of me.

Glimpse

Light catches the jam, your hand, between the fingers red,
placing the still warm jar on the shelf.
I can almost touch you, your face steamed pink
from the rolling boil, finger tips pricked; haw berry, quince,
deep purple brambles, staining your shoes,
back from your ramble, wind-blown home.

Progress Report

I'm just fishing,
though I don't have to stand thigh-high
in the chilly river to dangle my rod.
No hip books, but still I get my line tangled.
How can I put so many feet wrong,
when I'm wearing the same two as yesterday.

Who knows what I'll pull up today,
a tyre, Lucozade bottle, one mitten in Sanquhar pattern,
or the flying salmon that lands in my net.
Through the seasons of reason and unreasonableness,
I've fished, dry bed, rocky, sun stinging the eyes, high tide
when the brackish khaki brown foams itself with haste.

The fish swat my angles in their eagerness to be on their way.
Brushing past, some too close, nibbling at my dead skin,
Sorry, sorry, sorry, a chorus of fish as they swim off,
their voices bouncing between the trees,
ping pongs, pom poms. The ones that got away,
or went away to the deep end. I follow.

Mae West, talking to the Berries

I'd grow thorns if I was as beautiful as you,
bramble myself inaccessible,
each plump globule clinging to itself,
touched only by rain, bees, sun, wind,
shining in the light somewhere between black and purple.
I'd keep the taste of me to myself,
burst inwards, sweet, tart.

Interpreting the Recipe

I'm trying to get the fish to sit, slippery as it is;
the custard to stand,
meat to rest after it's long gallop in the oven;
the estranged couple called oil and vinegar, to marry,
dough to rise, wine to breathe.
Meanwhile, cooking blind, the milk goes off
and the cow jumps over the spoon.

Triste
(For Umberto)

I get distracted by the sound of the words.
For the word for *words*, see *parole,*
an ex-con out on parole.

I get distracted by Giancarlo's acoustic guitar,
forget I'm supposed to be doing something.
Giancarlo gets distracted by my words, forgets to play.

Light distracts me, dark, small wonders at my feet.
How to describe these combinations of colours,
Autumn's shower of leaves, senza parole.

Sometimes the absence of words distracts me,
silence soothes me, digging the rich soil,
forgetting I'm supposed to be sad.

Things That Trip Me Up

Yesterday it was his boots,
shaped to the bunion that sometimes hobbled him;
socks worn away at the heel, neatly rolled in a drawer.

Today it's a scrap of paper, flap of an envelope,
words that look like, *I love you,* though could be
two lemons, battery, something abbreviated.

The Dreich Elephant Speaks
(For Morag)

It's
very
pleasant
here,
when
it
forgets
to
rain.
It
just
so
seldom
does.

**

The rain has been kind today.
It waited to see the back of me,
key turning slowly in the lock of the swollen door,
wind turning droplets into dancers on the glass,
a ballet of frogs down my neck.

**

The Postman came late with his bag full of rain;
my water bill floating, soppy letters from the Sunshine State,
bold letters, declaring that I'd won something,
bleeding off the page.
Everything's gone green, tree trunks, fence, stone, me.

**

The smirrie rain smears my thoughts,
wet shoes, drookit socks.
The bailiffs are at my door, doun London;

it's about that car I don't have,
parking wrongly all over the city,
exceeding the limit in a Humping Zone;
small children, old sticks,
and this Jack Russell nipping at my heels,
cup of tea, coffee, yin of those plain biscuits,
and what about the others, you asked them, kin.

      **

I go to the hills because they won't come to me.
A green wave of long grasses I walk between.
They sway and wiggle a bit, but don't undulate,
or call to me, quite the way sea does.

      **

Today it's an I-don't-care-kind of rain.
It's out, I'm in my own bubble of thought.
We don't have to meet today.
Blessed be the rain that falls down upon the dead,
those starlets, angels on the pane.

That was the first time he knew that his mother knew poetry,
words passed down, not knowing who said it first.
Blessed be the rain I don't have to go out in.
It's good for the garden, the bulbs, the seeds,
the crowns of trees, lush and green the Galloway hills roll.

      **

In the journal of rain days, 365 are mentioned.
Barrels overflowed, threw themselves off crumbling cliffs.
Water ran and ran with nowhere to go. Frantic,
it jumped the step, sheltered in the shed, then found the house.
Thoughts floated along with the carpet.
Water, rising up sniffing for the sea,

blindly looking for the way back to the Solway.
Not even the bees were interested in the drowning petals.
No seeding, no ark, no two by two.

      **

It
took
me
two
years
to
dry
out,
wringe
this
heart
thru
the
Mangle

life
had
become.
And
still
I
say,
blessed
be
the
rain,
all
our
dead.

Time Keeping

Without the heart and all the senses, it's just reportage.
Up on Ward 10, down on 7, talking to X,
taking notes for Y in isolation, barely pausing on the stairs
to look at the tapestries of Sky, Earth, Sea.
In and out the Alex Unit, off to Kingholm Quay, Annan,
seeing A, B, C at home. Painting with words,
knitting, knitting, knitting in clinic, making endless cups of.
I'd anticipated getting calluses on my writing fingers,
not these dish pan hands. Was it 30 or 40 cups today,
washed, rinsed, dried.
So and so's funeral, such and such a piece of writing with D, E, F.
But it doesn't go like that and while you're brushing past
a field of bluebells, we're contemplating the wonder of just one,
the miracle of it all, how darkness so often gives way to light,
how the rain clears and everything glistens.
The last words weren't. There was so much more to say.
Can you hear it; so clear to me I answer.

In the Dark

Seven Sisters, and what happened to the brothers.
Ups and Downs, marshes,
then you know you've missed your stop, passed it.
The last of the light has lost your way
and there is no Way Out,
but to stay on this train
to its final destination.
Who knows, maybe you'll want to live here,
Stone, where the train doesn't stop.

After Frost

The arrows of our ways are always pointing
in the direction we might have taken,
ways we might have responded.
Things he gave her she never honoured,
how he didn't honour her reluctance to receive.
He didn't honour, she didn't honour
his acceptance, her rejection.
The little moments all too gone quickly.
Foxes now are fighting in the street,
digging up the window boxes.

Baton

I could be an Olympic runner,
the way I carry this torch for you.
But where do you want me to take it.
Which politician's backside
do you want me to light up,
as if fire could illuminate the truth.

Or should I just stop running towards the impossibility
that any of our voices make a difference.
Go instead to the void, light up the forest,
douse the flames in a loch I'm not locked into.
Take what remains of this flickering light,
to the thin places hoping.

Bushwacker

I'd write you a letter,
but I don't think we speak the same language.
Your definition of diplomacy,
differs from Mr. Webster's.
He says diplomacy is *about trying to get along.*
You say: *it's about winning.*
There are other differences; see Webster
on *freedom and democracy.*
Note: the d comes before the f.

Tripping

Even in his static state, pinned down to drips and oxygen tank,
he was travelling. His mind a rich tapestry of invention,
all he had for entertainment. Wales came into it,
then he was in Australia, working in factories, bakeries.

He insisted we all be silent as he was sure he was being interviewed
on the Kosovo border by the BBC. Forever worried about some
jacket left behind in the shuffle. *You know what it's like when
you move rooms in a hotel, something always gets left behind.*

The leather jerkin from his National Service days, the one he had on
when I met him; the one from his James Dean days.
The red one from ten Christmases ago. He floated between times,
eyes darting into hidden pockets of remembrance. Now, is a blank.

Getting Together
(for David Crystal)

What will we talk about next time
if we don't meet up this time,
even if it means a walk in August's pissing rain.
The garden that drew us to this pub, awash,
umbrellas folded like defeated birds, chairs stacked.
Every crack of thunder shudders us
as we wait for lightning to strike.
We must be mad, a block away from Tony's, but he
can't come and play because he's in South London where I live.
You're reminded of all the horrible holidays,
stuck in a caravan with parents who didn't get along.
The rain, the rain, the rain, rowing with itself.

Waking the Wildebeast

I had a dream,
wavering on the tip of remembrance
balancing on the tightrope edge of a poem
I could almost hear,
music I could almost see.

I was floating, floating
towards the kettle
towards the first coffee of the day,
precious silence, rare moment
before the self becomes itself.
Holding, holding so gently
to a hair of a thought, whisker of a colour

when you spoke.

Not the early morning song of a bird
I could weave into my dream,
but right brain speech I couldn't ignore,
right in my face, and I felt the dream slip away.
Sand poured through the hour glass,
then the glass broke
shattering me in your face.

Oh yes, then I was awake
but no longer myself.

Long Division

1.

I could stay here, at home in this new skin of myself;
known as someone I've never been before.
The shoes fit. They hold water.
But for how long in this weather.

I could re-invent my past, an only child, an orphan, a dolphin.
Not the Captain's daughter, always moving, port to port.
I could say I don't remember where I come from – Amnesia.
Forget about that house full of ghosts riffling through reams of paper.

Here, no one's looking over my shoulder for the one who isn't there.
I'm not the painful reminder, half the equation, poor substitute.
People here didn't know me when, or him, or elsewhere. Then again,
there's comfort in knowing those who are part of the history.

I'd get a dog and call it and call it,
and it wouldn't come, some goofy looking thing,
whose back legs don't match his front when he runs.
Or a pony, and I, put out to pasture in a bay of wind.

2.

Division lives in the nib of this pen, Go or stay.
Looking back, looking ahead. *Go, when you see the Green Man.*
I'm divided about that. There's always the other hand to consider,
if you have two, and the foxes haven't stolen all your shoes.

How quickly the unknown gets known, the landscape familiar:
Kippford, Rockcliffe, Kirkcudbright, Kirkmahoe, Kingholm Quay.
Castle Douglas where the wind always blows up the High Street.
The bus routes I know, the drivers, the fare, the timing of it all.

The little girl with the violin case, middle of nowhere. Near to
but not Sweetheart Abbey. Thornhill, Moffat, Langholm,, Dalbeattie,
Gatehouse, Bake House, Maxwelltown, Southerness, Sandy Hills,
Caerlaverock, and the Mull of Galloway I know. Puffins.

A grey-haired lady emerges from the mist, wicker basket on her arm.
Eggs she's taking to market to sell. I've stepped back in time. School
children play on a stone wall, the one with the ginger Mowhawk,
cheeky grin, drops my heart down to my socks remembering my son.

3.

I don't even have to be thinking about you. Minding my own
thoughts, walking down the cobbled town, eating my apple,
past the statue of Burns, glance at the Midsteeple Clock.
Will I be late or early. It's only when I go to throw the core away
that I feel your hand on my shoulder, your words in my mouth.
Don't throw that away, that's the best part.
The core? What are you, a horse?
No, we were just poor. The heart of it all.

Sometimes it's the aggravation I miss,
that gristy criticism about something I've got on,
back of my hair, something I'm doing wrong.
I wish you wouldn't do that.
I only do it when I want to conjure the exasperation in your voice.
Otherwise, I use the cutting board.
There's no one here,
 to nag me to pick up this, shuffle that, move over.
Just you at the core, wherever I go.

4.

I let my eyes get lost on the way, following the coast.
The Belties I know. Sheep I bleat back at.
Marion, Mary, Susan, Sandra, Dee…I have to say their names,
the dead I knew: Helen, John, Jim, Joe, Colin, Donald.
Leave space, there are more… Heather…

Their voices, their stories, their faces, clearer than my own.
I dart past the shock of my reflection in the mirror.
The one who got Sudokued, rubber shavings round her chair.
Laughter filters through it all, such brief and not so, encounters.
Home, I hear myself call this place; these people family.

5.

The key finding its way in the lock,
me knowing how the door will knock into the wall in the wind.
Home, this minimalist nest I've managed to cram full.
One suitcase in, ten boxes out.
Coldest flat on earth, Bernadette says,
rubbing her hands like a raccoon.
Visitors never take their hats and coats off.

I sleep in outdoor gear, socks, fleece, hat with flaps, and mittens.
Radio 4 finds its way into my dreams.
The frost that is my breath wakes me saying, *Shut Up.*
The bathroom's so small I have to go in sideways, a tub I fold into
numbing myself with scalding water. My tub. My candles. My wine.
My paint work. My plants in pots on the gravel. This rented space.

The dark green carpet in the sitting room leads me to the outside.
Criffel, other side of the river in a golden halo.

Hills light up for a moment, before sun devours them
giving way to darkness, stars.
Everything is just for a moment, hold it.

6.

Such big veins, I hear Nurse Hazel say.
I know that glint in her eye.
She wants to practice canulation on me.
I keep her busy making a pom pom out of string.
Maybe it's time to leave the too familiar.
Go or stay, either way, half of me will be left behind.
Ghosts wherever I go, and that's just life.
One of ours is always missing,
and, never very far away.
No place is neutral.

Threads

My sister wanted to clear his clothes,
as if it would dispel my grief,
erase the pain she couldn't bear to see.
She dove into the closet, into his pockets.
Dead trousers destined for the place where dead trousers go,
the painting ones, the tan ones, blue striped
from the just painted bench whose sign blew away in the wind.
Shirts with arms hanging off,
pockets askew that he refused to have mended.
Not the shirt so much that I want to preserve,
but the way he wore it through to thread,
bare and bold with it, every piece a story to be told.

In Answer to Your Question
(for Roy Fisher)

I'm making split pea soup,
ham knuckle,
that's what I'm doing.

I'm hanging one green, one red towel
on the clothesline
in my blue garden.

I'm packing my bags,
checking my ticket again and again,
not trusting myself.

I'm sitting in The Woodlands,
waiting for a thought I've never had before.
Waiting, waiting through bird song, rattle of leaves.

Things to do today

Empty myself of the fullness of myself,
fill myself with the little time left,
do something useful.
Plant the black tulip bulbs in the blue pots.
Fill in the fox hole.
Make lemon bread for someone I love.

So It Goes

Bring
on
the
dull
days,
edge
of
Mull
days,
old
ways
we
struggle
to

return
to,
and
I'll
tell
you
why
the
ivy
twines,
rampaging
through
the
forest.

Nature
is
my
nurture.
See
how
I
pretty
up
the
flowers
for
the
bees.

Something
bright,
Mamma
always
said.
My
petal,
my
poppet.
Not
just
a
pretty
face.

What I Know

It
takes
the
time
it
takes
to
peel
back
what
was
life,
when
gone.

Transition

Another part of my life goes through the door.
Sun without the light,
distilled without water,
caught between where going, where been,
how to speak about it.

I go to the pockets of life and hem myself in,
drugged by wind into submission,
changed by change, chanced by chances taken, missed.
It's the little choices we make that change our lives;
not turning the light on, missing the last step.

Leisure

Today I will go swim,
not round and round in goldfish fashion
but up and down in orderly lanes
amongst the splashers, the flailers, the guppies,
and the one who causes a tidal wave trying to do the Butterfly.
It's good for me I say
and then think with dismay how I leisure myself
using more water than some villages have in a year.
Each drop I spit out is someone's lifeline.
If we could just tip the earth
the way one tips a pitcher,
fill the empty from the too full.

Travel Plans

I'll
just
stay
still
for
now,
let
clouds
be
the
movement
in
my
life.